BAYERN

From the Königssee to Neuschwanstein
Castle and on to Lake Constance

Desde Königssee al Castillo de
Neuschwanstein hasta el Lago de Costanza

Introduction

This book is an illustrated volume which aims to introduce the beauties and sights of Upper Bavaria. It does not claim to give a detailed description of the region. The texts are mainly designed to give you an idea about the area and provide some introductory information. If you would like to know more about the area between the Königssee and Lake Constance, we recommend a detailed guide book. However, if you just want to show your friends and relations at home where you spent your holidays, or to get an idea of what the region's like, this book's for you.

The beautiful part of Bavaria between the Königssee and Lake Constance featured in this book is situated in the area of the Pre-Alps and Alps, and mainly comprises the administrative districts of Upper Bavaria and Allgäu.

It is bounded to the east by the River Salzach and to the south by the German-Austrian border; to the west it extends as far as Lake Constance.

Bavaria is considered to be one of the most ancient regions of Europe. It is interesting to note that some areas, such as the Berchtesgaden and Chiemgau regions, have only belonged to Bavaria since the early 19th century. At that time the dynasty of the Wittelsbachs, the most powerful ruling family in Bavaria, had centuries of domination behind it and one more in front of it, as the family's rule only ended with the First World War in 1918.

In 1871, after the Franco-Prussian War, the Kingdom of Bavaria joined the German Empire as a federal state. Five years earlier, Bavarian troops had fought side by side with the Austrians against the Prussians, who then accelerated the union of Lesser Germany, excluding Austria. There is still some resentment between Bavarians and Prussians today, which dates back to the time of this more or less voluntary annexation.

As a result of the economic development of Upper Bavaria as well as its predominant agriculture, trade between Northern Italy and the business towns of Augsburg and Nuremberg has been very important for centuries. However, in many parts of the more mountainous regions, agriculture did not provide a sufficient living, so the inhabitants turned their attention to second jobs, including goods haulage, crafts, outwork and rock salt mining. In the 19th century industrialisation only became established in Munich, Augsburg and Rosenheim, whereas in the other areas of Upper Bavaria, tourism became increasingly important.

Its natural beauties made Upper Bavaria the most popular holiday area in Germany. The court, nobility, senior clergymen, and later the bourgeoisie sought peace and quiet there. The increasing number of visitors and structures created to accommodate them eventually necessitated the introduction of environmental protection measures. Various large nature reserves have now been created to protect the wild life.

The area between the Königssee and Lake Constance has much more to offer than its beautiful landscape; a multitude of winter and summer sports facilities, artistic and cultural events and numerous sights. The visitor often follows in the footsteps of the Wittelsbach King Ludwig II (1845-1886) whose lavish building projects incurred large debts and alienated the government; however, this legacy now brings cash pouring into the coffers of the State Castles Board.

The fairytale king, who ascended to the Bavarian throne at the age of 18, escaped as often as he could from both court life and the common people, leaving the royal residence in Munich for the poetic refuges he had built in the most beautiful areas; on the Chiemsee and the Walchensee, in the Karwendel, Wetterstein and Ammer mountains he lived in a mediaeval dream world in his chalets, fortresses and castles.

This is not the place to describe every aspect of the numerous landscapes of Upper Bavaria. A whole book would not suffice to describe all the woods, lakes, mountains and rivers in the Bavarian Alps and Pre-Alps. The same applies to the wild life, which brings more joy and pleasure to some tourists than the most beautiful Rococo churches and Baroque castles.

Those who also want to get to know the population of Upper Bavaria would do well to visit not only the tourist areas, but also the smaller towns where, in many places, folk festivals are still celebrated which are by no means staged only for tourists. Some examples are the Festival of St. Leonard, Corpus Christi and Carnival. In Bavaria, "folk festival" means just that: everyone takes part, young and old, rich and poor alike. The same applies to the numerous open-air beer gardens which are an essential feature of every Bavarian town.

Many visitors to Upper Bavaria will want to go on to Lake Constance.

In Füssen and the nearby royal castles we are no longer in the ethnic Bavarian part of Bavaria but the Swabian part - the Bavarian Allgäu. The landscape becomes gentler and hillier, the settlements show a strong agricultural influence, and the inhabitants differ from the ethnic Bavarians of Upper Bavaria not only in terms of dialect, but also in their lifestyle, customs and festivals. However, there is certainly no lack of sights and art treasures in the Bavarian Allgäu, and tourism is just as important here as in Upper Bavaria.

Perhaps this book will persuade you to return or, if you've never been to this area, to spend your next holiday there. In any case, we hope you've enjoyed reading it.

Introducción

Este libro es un volumen ilustrado que entiende presentaros las bellezas y los monumentos de la Alta Baviera. No pretende tanto ofrecer una descripción detallada cuanto dar una idea y proporcionar al lector algunas informaciones sobre esta región. Si deseáis datos más precisos sobre la región situada entre Königssee y el Lago de Costanza os aconsejamos una guía turística detallada. Pero, si queréis ilustrar a quien se ha quedado en casa donde habéis transcurrido vuestras vacaciones o si queréis haceros sólo una idea de esta región, habéis hecho la justa elección.

La bella Baviera situada entre Königssee y el Lago de Costanza que os presentamos en este libro se encuentra en el territorio de los Prealpes y de los Alpes y comprende sustancialmente las circunscripciones administrativas de la Alta Baviera y del Allgäu.

Está delimitada al este por el Salzach, al sur por la frontera austriaca y al oeste se extiende hasta el Lago de Costanza.

Baviera está considerada como una de las regiones más antiguas de Europa. Es interesante constatar que algunas de sus zonas - como la región de Berchtesgaden y Chiemgau - pertenecen a Baviera sólo desde el siglo XIX. En este periodo, la dinastía de los Wittelsbacher, la estirpe de reyes más poderosa de Baviera, tenía a sus espaldas ya algunos siglos de dominio - y aún uno por delante. De hecho la dominación de los Wittelsbacher terminó en 1918, al final de la primera Guerra Mundial. En 1871 el Reino de Baviera - después de la guerra entre alemanes y franceses - se unió al Imperio Prusiano como estado federal. Cinco años antes, las tropas bavaresas habían luchado junto con los austriacos contra los prusianos, que más tarde aceleraron la unión de la Pequeña Alemania sin Austria.

Algunos de los resentimientos existentes aún hoy entre bavareses y prusianos tienen su origen en el periodo de esta anexión más o menos voluntaria.

Al desarrollo económico de la Alta Baviera, además de la agricultura predominante, el comercio entre Italia Septentrional y las ciudades comerciales de Augusta y Nuremberg ha contribuido durante siglos, jugando siempre un papel muy importante. Sin embargo, en muchas ciudades de las regiones más montañosas, la agricultura no era suficiente como actividad vital, por lo que el hombre ha tenido que dedicarse a trabajos secundarios como transporte de mercancías, artesanía, trabajos a domicilio, extracción de sal gema. Durante el siglo XIX, en la Alta Baviera, la industria consiguió imponerse sólo en Mónaco, Augusta y Rosenheim, mientras que en las demás zonas ha tomado siempre mayor importancia el turismo.

Han sido las bellezas naturales las que han hecho de la Alta Baviera el territorio más frecuentado de Alemania para transcurrir las vacaciones. La corte, la nobleza, el alto clero y más tarde incluso la burguesía, han buscado aquí paz y tranquilidad. El creciente número de huéspedes y por consiguiente de las estructuras creadas para acogerlos, ha hecho necesario tomar medidas para salvaguardar el ambiente. Hoy algunos parques naturales se han convertido en el refugio de la flora y la fauna.

Además de un paisaje bello y encantador, la región situada entre Königssee y el Lago de Costanza presenta muchos otros atrativos: se pueden practicar numerosas actividades deportivas invernales y veraniegas, asistir a manifestaciones artísticas y culturales y visitar numerosos monumentos. En esta región nos encontramos muchas veces sobre la pista del noble Ludwig II Wittelsbach (1845-1886) que con su pródiga actividad edilicia se llenó de deudas, atrayendo la ira del gobierno. Hoy, por el contrario, la Administración del Estado de los castillos, trae grandes beneficios de las obras construida por este rey.

El Rey de los cuentos que en 1864, a 18 años, subió al trono bavarés, escapaba cada vez que le era posible de la ciudad residencial de Mónaco, de la vida de la corte e incluso del pueblo común, para refugiarse en las romanticas demoras que había hecho construir en las más bellas localidades: sobre los lagos Chiemsee y Walchensee, entre las montañas de Karwendel, Wetterstein y Ammer. En estos refugios, fortalezas y castillos vivía en un mundo fantastico medieval.

No queremos describir aquí en todos sus aspectos la multiplicidad de los paisajes de la Alta Baviera. En realidad no bastaría un libro para describir los bosques, los lagos, las montañas y los rios de la zona de los Alpes y de los Prealpes bavareses. Lo mismo vale para la flora y la fauna, que a algunos turistas proporciona más alegría y más placer que las estupendas iglesias rococó y los castillos barrocos.

Aquellos que deseen conocer también la población de la Alta Baviera, deberían visitar no sólo las localidades turísticas, sino también los pueblos más pequeños, en la mayor parte de los cuales, se celebran aún fiestas populares como la Fiesta de San Leonardo, el Corpus Dómini o el Carnaval, fiestas que no son sólo organizadas para los turistas. En Baviera, las fiestas populares no lo son sólo de nombre, pues a ellas participan jóvenes, ancianos, ricos y pobres. Lo mismo ocurre con las numerosas cervecerías al aire libre, que son una parte integrante de cada pueblo bavarés.

Muchos visitantes de la Alta Baviera no renunciarán seguramente a continuar hasta el Lago de Costanza.

En Füssen y en los cercanos castillos reales el territorio ya no es bávaro, estamos en la parte sueca de Baviera: en el Allgäu Bavarés. El paisaje es más dulce y con colinas, los asentamientos demuestran una fuerte orientación agrícola y las personas se diferencian de los bavareses meridionales bávaros, sea por el dialecto, que por el modo de vivir, las costumbres y las fiestas populares. De todas maneras en el Allgäu Bavarés no faltan ciertamente los monumentos y los tesoros artísticos, también aquí, el turismo juega un papel importante como en la Alta Baviera.

Quizás este guía podrá induciros a volver a esta tierra o, si aún no la conocéis, a transcurrir aquí las próximas vacaciones. En cualquiera de los casos deseamos que este libro resulte una lectura agradable.

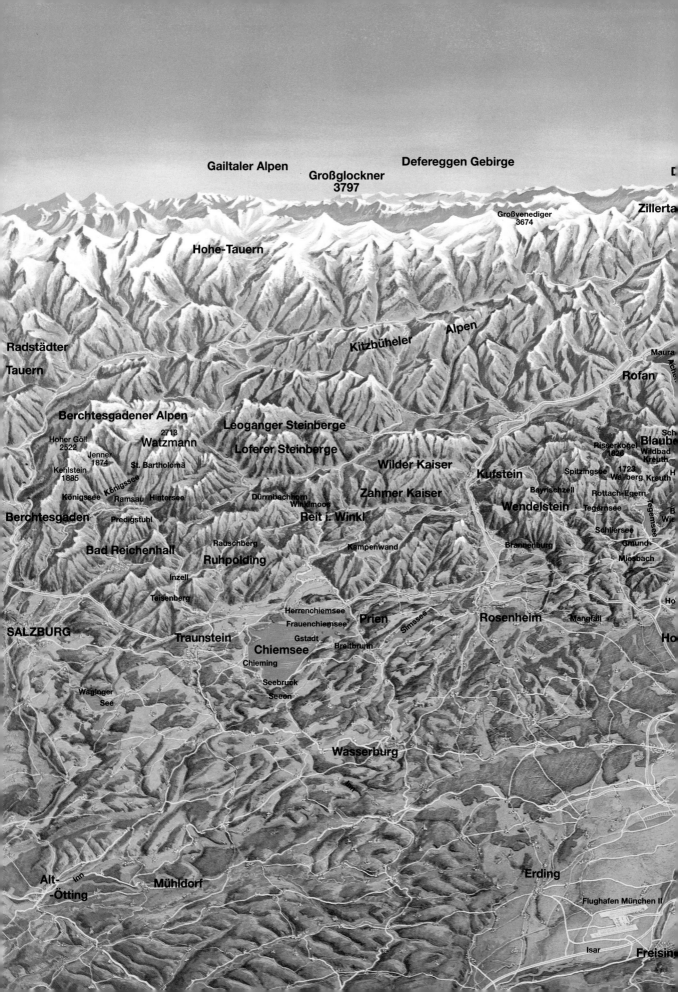

Munich

Munich

Munich, the heart of the Bavarian highland, is the capital and economic center of gravity of Bavaria. The settlement nucleus, founded in the eighth century by the monks of the Benedictine Cloister in Tegernsee – the name Munich comes from the phrase *at the monks'* – began to develop, starting in the twelfth century, thanks to its position at the intersection of the most important east-west and north-south nexuses, until it became a market and trade center. From the thirteenth century on, Munich was the residence of the House of Wittelsbach, the most important Bavarian dynasty.

Not only its position as a traffic junction but also its role as the Court Residence contributed to the prominence of Munich. On the one hand, il is the third most important industral city in the Federal Republic, with its famous electronic industries, its machinery and vehicle factories, arnaments industry and, by no means last, its six gigantic beer factories. On the other, it has been since the reign of Ludwig I (1825-1848), one of the leading art centers of Europe and one of the beacons of the spiritual life of southern Germany. This is attested to not only by the numerous museums, galleries, theaters, universities and institutes that throng Munich but also by the more than 300 publishing firms, printing works, motion-picture studios as well as photographers and moviemakers.

Of course, Munich too, a city which is regularly invaded by hordes of tourists, has much to offer its guests – and not only in the fall, when the **Oktoberfest** draws city-dwellers, both young and old, and guests from all over the world to the *Wiesn*. Anyone with cultural interests, for example, will find, in addition to the structures already mentioned, a host of buildings of interest from the old **City Gates** to the **Frauenkirche** and from the old and new Marienplatz Town Hall to the ornament-laden **Asamkirche** and on, still further, to modern works like the 1972 Olympic Center with its famous plastic tent cover and the olympic tower. Seen from the Olympiaberg, the Frauenkirche seems to be nestled, especially when the *Föhn* wafts in, at the feet of the Zugspitze, which is nearly 100 kilometers (63 miles) away.

For strollers who love to wander around and look at everything, there are, besides the center of the city with its pedestrian precincts and **Food Market**, the Embankment of the Isar River, the English Garden and, of course, the elegant shop windows along the Leopoldstrasse in the Schwabinger district. Other parts of the city which have kept their own, unique character are, for example, the Haidhausen, Neuhausen and **Nymphenburg** districts.

Munich, corazón del altiplano bávaro, es la capital y el centro de gravedad económico de la Baviera. El núcleo habitativo, fundado en el siglo octavo por los monjes del claustro benedictino de Tegernsee – el nombre Munich trae su origen de *junto a los monjes* – empezó a desarrollarse a partir del siglo duodécimo gracias a su ubicación en la intersección de las más importantes vías de comunicación este-oeste y norte-sur, hasta volverse un centro mercantil y comercial. Allende esto, desde el siglo décimotercero Munich se ha volvido la residencia de los Wittelsbacher, la dinastía bávara, la más importante.

Quiera su ubicación, como nudo de traficación, quiera su función, como Residencia de Corte, han contribuído a la importancia de Munich actual: de un lado es la tercera ciudad industrial en orden de importancia de la República Federal de Alemania, con sus célebres industrias electrotécnicas, las fábricas de maquinarias y de vehículos, la industria de los armamentos y, no últimas, sus seis gigantescas fábricas de cerveza, y, de otro lado, desde el época del reino de Ludovico I (1825-1845), es un centro de arte de importancia europea y uno de los puntos firmes de la vida espiritual de la Alemania del Sur. Son testimonio de esta realidad no solamente los numerosos museos, las galerías, los teatros, las universidades y los Institutos Superiores, mas también los más de 300 editores, imprentas, estudios cinematográficos y productores fotográficos y cinematográficos, que contribuyen todos ellos a la importancia de Munich como centro de *Media*.

Naturalmente, también Munich, ciudad de intenso tránsito turístico, tiene algo a ofrecer a sus huéspedes – y no sólo en el otoño, cuando la **Oktoberfest** ve afluir los ciudadanos jóvenes y viejos y los huéspedes de todo el mundo al barrio *Wiesn*.

Por ejemplo, los que tienen intereses culturales hallan, allende las estructuras antedichas, muchas maravillas arquitectónicas, desde las antiguas **Puertas de la Ciudad** a la **Frauenkirche**, desde el viejo y nuevo Ayuntamiento de Marienplatz a la exuberante y ornamental **Asamkirche**, hasta las obras modernas, cuales el Centro Olímpico de 1972, con su famosa cobertura de plástica hecha como una tienda y la torre olímpica.

Para quienes aman callejear y mirarse alrededor, existen, además del centro de la ciudad con sus zonas para peatones y el **Mercado Alimenticio**, también el Lungo-Isar y los **Jardines Británicos** y, naturalmente, los quilómetros de vitrinas elegantes a lo largo de la Leopoldstrasse, en el barrio de Schwabing. Mas también otros sectores de la ciudad han mantenido intacta su peculiar característica, como, por ejemplo, los barrios de: Haidhausen, Neuhausen y Nymphenburg.

Munich: Town Hall belltower with the Pillar of Mary

Mónaco: Carillón de la torre del Municipio con columna mariana.

Plate 1: View from Föhnwind: Munich with the Alpine range
Plates 2 and 3: The famous Hofbräuhaus with its beer garden.
Plate 4: The Chinese tower in the English Garden
Plate 5: Nymphenburg castle
Plate 6: Marienplatz with the Frauenkirche (Church of Our Lady) and the new Town Hall
Plate 7: Ludwigstrasse and the "Schwabing" begin at the Siegestor (Victory Gate)

Figura 1: Panorama de Föhnwind: Mónaco con la cadena de los Alpes.
Figuras 2 y 3: La famosa cervecería de corte con su zona al aire libre.
Figura 4: La torre china en el Englischer Garten.
Figura 5: El Castillo de Nymphenburg.
Figura 6: La Marienplatz con la Frauenkirche y el Nuevo Municipio.
Figura 7: A la Siegestor empiezan la Ludwigstraße y "Schwabing".

7

The Oktoberfest

The Oktoberfest, inextricably linked with Munich, has been celebrated at Theresienwiese every year since 1810 with processions, brass band music and beer tents, and attracts 100,000 visitors.

Inseparable de Mónaco es el Oktoberfest, que desde 1810 se festeja cada año en Theresienwiese con festivos cortejos, músicas con instrumentos de aire y grandes telones convertidos en cervecerías con la participación de cien mil visitantes.

Plate 1: Brass band music at the Bavaria
Plate 2: Brewer's dray in the procession
Plate 3: Under the marquee

Figura 1: Música con instrumentos de aire en la Bavaria
Figura 2: Carro de la cerveza durante el cortejo.
Figura 3: Bajo el telón de la cerveza.

Augsburg

The former name "Augustus Burg" alludes to the ancient foundation of the city by the Romans in 11 B.C. From a "splendissima colonia" it grew to become the "Golden Augsburg" of the Middle Ages. Augsburg owed this flourishing period to the commercial skills of the Welser and Fugger families. The Fuggers in particular not only gave the city costly buildings, but were also great patrons of all the arts and artists of the day. Today, as well as being a commercial and industrial city, Augsburg has remained a centre for art and culture.

◆

El nombre de "Augustus Burg" alude a la antigua fundación por parte de los romanos en el año 11 antes de Cristo. Desde la "Esplendida Colonia" a la "Augusta Dorada" de la Edad Media. Augusta debe este periodo floreciente a la habilidad comercial de los Welser y de los Fugger. Sobre todo, los Fugger regalaron a la ciudad no sólo preciosas construcciones sino que fueron también grandes mecenas de todos los tipos de arte y de todos los artistas de la época. Además de una ciudad comercial e industrial, Augsburgo es, aún hoy, un centro artístico y cultural.

Plate 1: South portal of Gothic chancel of the Cathedral
Plate 2: In the Fuggerei
Plate 3: Cathedral windows
Plate 4: The Perlach Tower behind the Town Hall. On the right is St. Ulrich's Cathedral, and on the far right, the Maximilian Museum
Plate 5: Town Hall Square with the Augustus Fountain
Plate 6: Augsburg Cathedral: 10th-15th centuries

Figura 1: Portal sur del coro gótico de la Catedral.
Figura 2: En la Fuggerei.
Figura 3: Vidrieras de la Catedral.
Figura 4: La Torre Perlach, detrás del Municipio, a la derecha la Catedral de San Ulrico y más a la derecha el museo de Maximiliano.
Figura 5: La Plaza del Municipio con la Fuente de Augusto.
Figura 6: La Catedral de Augsburgo (siglos X - XV).

5

6

The Land of Five Lakes

The Starnbergersee, Ammersee, Wörthsee, Pilsensee and Wesslingersee are the enchanting bodies of water for which the Land of Five Lakes, situated in the southwestern region of Munich, is named. The biggest of the five is the Starnbergersee (57.2 km2), the spot preferred by sailing, surfing and other water-sports fans. However, admirers of the Bavarian king, Ludwig II (1845-1886), also come here to the Isle of Roses, where Kini spent hours that were shrouded in mystery with his cousin Sissy, the Empress of Austria. Ludwig ended his days here on the 13th of June, two days after his disqualification and dismissal. He drowned in the waters of the lake in front of the **Schlossberg**, together with his psychiatrist. It is still not known whether or not he committed suicide, and a cross stands in the water where he died while, on the shore there is a commemorative chapel. The Ammersee is also worth a visit, if only for the interesting Andechs Monastery on the "Holy Mount" above the Ammersee; its complex consisting of church, monastery buildings and small brewery is not only a classic place of pilgrimage but also a favourite spot for outings.

The ancient Bavarian town of **Weilheim** (right of town since 1236), situated near the Starnbergersee and the Ammersee, is also worth a visit.

◆

El Starnbergersee, el Ammersee, el Wörthsee, el Pilsensee y el Wesslingersee dan el nombre a la tierra de los cinco lagos situada en la región sur occidental de Munich. El mayor de los cinco es el lago de Starnbergersee (57,2 km2), meta preferida por los apasionados de vela, de surf, de natación de los demás deportes de agua. Pero, a este lago llegan también los admiradores del rey bávaro Ludwig II (1845-1886): aqui, en la isla de las Rosas, Kini (era su sobrenombre) había transcurrido horas envueltas en el misterio con la prima, la emperatriz de Austria Sissi, aqui, también, ha concluído sus días el 13 de junio de 1886, dos dias después de su interdicción y destitución, anegó en las aguas del lago del **castillo de Berg**, junto con su psiquiatra. Si se ha tratado de suicidio, aún hoy dia no es claro. En el lugar de la muerte hoy surge del agua una cruz y, en la plaza, hay una capilla conmemorativa. También el Ammersee es digno de una visita, aunque sólo sea por el interesante Convento Andechs que en la "Montaña Sagrada", sobre Ammersee, con el complejo constituido por la iglesia, el edificio del convento, la pequeña cervecería, no es sólo un lugar de peregrinaje sino también una meta muy amada para realizar excursiones. Merece también un salto la antigua ciudad bavaresa de **Weilheim** situada en las cercanías de Starnbergersee y de Ammersee.

Large photo: the King Ludwig II memorial cross at Berg Castle on the Starnbergersee
Small photos:
Plate 1: The town of Weilheim
Plate 2: Andechs Monastery on the Ammersee
Plate 3: Boat trip on the Starnbergersee
Plate 4: Ilkarhöhe with the Starnbergersee
Plate 5: On the Ammersee

Figura Grande: La cruz conmemorativa del Rey Ludwig II en el Castillo de Berg sobre el Starnbergersee.
Figuras pequeñas:
Figura 1: Ciudad de Weilheim.
Figura 2: El Convento de Andechs en Ammersee.
Figura 3: Vuelta en lancha en el Starnbergersee.
Figura 4: Illkarhöhe y el Starnbergersee.
Figura 5: En el Ammersee.

3

4

5

The Region of Berchtesgaden

In the southeast corner of Upper Bavaria, surrounded to a great extent by the Austrian federal state of Salzburg, lies the region of Berchtesgaden – a valley encompassed and protected by tall mountains which, dating from the period of its colonization in the twelfth century, maintained its independence up until 1810 under the direct command of a prince of the Church. It was only in that year that it was annexed to the kingdom of Bavaria. The inhabitants of the area, however, had always had their *king* – the legendary **Watzmann**, 2,713 meters high, whose awesome eastern face is the highest in the Eastern Alps.

At the foot of this giant – in the heart of a natural park teeming with the most varied species of trees and plants to be seen anywhere – is the little baroque church of **Saint Bartholomew**, which can be reached by taking a silent, thermoelectrically-propelled ship across the picturesque **Königsee**. Those who love beautiful views don't have to scale Mt. Watzmann. All they have to do is travel up the Mautstrasse until they get to Rossfeld or pay a visit to Ramsau in the angle between Berchtesgaden and Reit im Winkel. Among these scenic areas there is one that is tied to a cataclysmic past – **Adolph Hitler's Teahouse** on the Obersalzberg.

The mercantile community of **Berchtesgaden**, famous health resort and winter sports center, is situated at the center of the valley. The inhabitants of this district capital make their living today mainly from tourism. Only a few still work in the rock salt mines, which for centuries represented the principal source of income for the people in the area. Today, visitors can go into the old mines and take a boat-ride over the subterranean salt lakes. Another means of earning a living in the old days, the art of wood-carving (*Berchtesgadner War*), is just managing to survive today. Worth a visit, too, are the **Stiftskirche** and the **Schlossmuseum**, where valuable works of art belonging to the House of Wittelsbach have been preserved. Moreover, in this comparatively isolated countryside, various characteristic customs have been kept intact, from the Palm Sunday Procession to the shooting matches on New Year's and the Advent *Buttnmandllaufen*.

Those who spend their vacations in the Berchtesgaden region should not pass up the opportunity to take some important excursions. **Salzburg** with its Festival and the spa at **Bad Reichenhall** with its celebrated mineral springs are only 30 kilometers away.

La Región de Berchtesgaden

En el ángulo sur-oriental de Baviera, circundada en grande parte por el Estado federal de Salisburgo, hállase la región de Berchtesgaden: una esclusa pantanosa circundada y protegida por altas montañas que, a partir del periodo de su colonización en el siglo duodécimo, se ha conservado independiente hasta el 1810 en calidad de prepositura principesca inmediata y solamente entonces fue anexa al reino de Baviera.

Los habitantes de la zona desde siempre tuvieron su *rey*, el legendario **Watzmann**, de 2713 metros de altura, cuya imponente pared este es la más alta de los Alpes Orientales.

A los pies de este gigante encuéntrase, en el corazón de un parque natural rico de la más variadas especies de plantas, la pequeña iglesia barroca de **San Bartolomé**, que puede ser alcanzada con un silencioso electro-buque que atraviesa el pintoresco Königsee. Quien ama las bellas vista panorámicas no tiene la necesidad de escalar la región de Berchtesgaden, como el monte Watzmann, es suficiente una gira en la Mautstrasse hasta Rossfeld o una visita a Ramsau en el ángulo que se queda entre Berchtesgaden y Reit i. Winkl. Entre estas zonas panorámicas, hay una que llama a la memoria trágicos recuerdos: la **Teehaus Adolf Hitlers** en el Obersalzberg.

La comunidad mercantil de **Berchtesgaden**, célebre estación climática y centro de deportes invernales, es ubicada en el Centro de la esclusa pantanosa. Los habitantes de esta ciudad, capital del distrito, hoy día viven en prevalencia de turismo.

Solo algunos todavía trabajan en las minas de sal gema, que por muchos siglos habían representado la principal fuente de recursos económicos para la población local.

Hoy día, los visitantes pueden hacer visita a las viejas minas y recorrer en bote los lagos salados subterráneos. También otra fuente de recursos de otros tiempos, el arte de entallar la madera (*Berchtesgadners War*), sobrevive como puede.

Merecen también una visita la **Stiftskirche** y el Schossmuseum, en donde hállanse custodiadas preciosas obras de arte de los Wittelsbacher.

Además, en tal paisaje, relativamente cerrado, se han conservado diversos usos y costumbres muy característicos, desde la Procesión del Domingo de Ramos, a los concursos de tiro del Primero de Año, a las *Buttnmandllaufen* del Adviento.

Quien desea transcurrir sus vacaciones en la región de Berchtesgaden, ne debe perder la oportunidad de hacer algunas importantes excursiones – **Salisburgo** con su Festival y la estación termal de **Bad Reichenhall** con sus caldas hidrominerales se quedan apenas a 30 quilómetros de distancia.

Large photo on p. 19: St. Bartholomew on the Königssee
Small photos:
left: Edelweiss
right: Chamois deer in the Berchtesgaden National Park

Figura grande de la página 19: San Bartolomeo en el Königssee.
Figuras pequeñas:
a la izquierda: Edelweiß.
a la derecha: Antílopes en el Parque Nacional de Berchtesgaden.

Large photo: Berchtesgaden with Mt. Watzmann (2713 m)
Small photos:
Plates 1 and 2: Rock salt mine
Plate 3: View from Mt. Jenner over the Königssee
Plate 4: Königssee, a picturesque corner
Plate 5: Königssee, landing stage

Figura grande: Berchtesgaden con el Watzmann (2713 m.).
Figuras pequeñas:
Figuras 1 y 2: Minas de sal gema.
Figura 3: Vista del Jenner sobre el Königssee.
Figura 4: Königssee, ángulo pintoresco.
Figura 5: Königssee, atracadero para las lanchas.

Top: Maria Gern near Berchtesgaden, looking towards Mt. Untersberg (1840 m)
Centre: Ramsau near Berchtesgaden
Bottom left: Berchtesgaden pedestrian precinct
Bottom right: On Rossfeld

Figura arriba: María Gern en Berchtesgaden, hacia Untersberg (1840 m.).
Figura central: Ramsau en Berchtesgaden.
Figura abajo a la izquierda: Berchtesgaden, zona peatonal.
Figura abajo a la derecha: Sobre el Roßfeld.

Top: *Berchtesgaden with Watzmann (2713 meters)*
Centre: *Kehlsteinhaus*
Bottom left: *Kehlsteinstrasse*
Bottom right: *The Hintersee with Höher Göll (2522 m)*

Figura arriba: Berchtesgaden con Watzmann (2713 m)
Figura central: Kehlsteinhaus.
Figura abajo a la izquierda: Kehlsteinstrasse.
Figura abajo a al derecha: Hintersee con Hoher Göll (2522 m.).

Salzburg and Bad Reichenhall

Large photo: Bad Reichenhall with the Predigtstuhl-cable car
Small photos:
Plate 1: Getreidegasse in Salzburg
Plate 2: Salzburg, the Festival town, with the Höhensalzburg-
on-Salzach fortress
Plate 3: Crucifix at Bad Reichenhall
Plate 4: Bad Reichenhall: main square with Town Hall
Plate 5: Bad Reichenhall park with portico

Figura grande: Bad Reichenhall con el funicular del Predigtstuhl.
Figuras pequeñas:
Figura 1: Getreidegasse en Salisburgo.
Figura 2: Salisburgo, la Ciudad del Festival con la Fortaleza Hohensalzburg en el Salzach.
Figura 3: Crucifijo en Bad Reichenhall.
Figura 4: Bad Reichenhall - Plaza principal con el Municipio.
Figura 5: Parque de Bad Reichenhall con soportal.

The Chiemgau region

Like berchtesgaden, Chiemgau forms part of those districts of Upper Bavaria which were annexed to the Kingdom of Bavaria only at the beginning of the nineteenth century. Previously, the region that surrounds the biggest lake in Bavaria had been under the political, religious and cultural influence of the diocese of Salzburg and its convents. The economic situation in Chiemgau was bolstered, in the main. as was agriculture, by the transportation of salt from Bad Reichenhall, before it was discovered that Chiemsee and the Chiemgau Alps had been found to be restful holiday resorts.

The *Bayerisches Meer*, which spreads out over 84.5 square kilometers, owes its popularity not only to its ideal position on the east-west intersection between Salzburg and Munich, its perfect conditions for water sports and mild climate – the lake acts as a heat accumulator in winter and on summer nights, thus levelling out wide fluctuations in temperature – but also to a number of famous sights located on and in the lake. From the Prien spa for the Kneipp cure, the *Chiemseebähnle* takes visitors to the port, where they then board steamers to go over to two large islands, which gave their names to the two cloisters of **Frauenwörth** and **Herrenwörth**. However, while the nuns' convent still exists on the *Fraueninsel* – the Gasthaus of the convent and the liqueur offered to guests are famous – the *Herreninsel* supplies an entirely different type of attraction – the **Neues Schloss**, a reconstruction of the Palace at Versailles, which Ludwig II started having built in 1878. The monument to the Bourbon King, Louis XIV, and his ideas as regards absolutism were never carried out, and the sovereign never used his sumptuous bed in the *Parade Bedroom* . Nevertheless, the more tham 600,000 tourists who visit the castle every year seem to be able to form an idea of Ludwig's imaginary world.

Less spectacular but more restful is the **hinterland** of Chiemsee – for example, the ponds like Klostersee with its **Seeon** cloister, the **Hohenaschau** Castle at the foot of the **Kampenwand** or the Chiemgau triangle made up of **Inzell**, **Ruhpolding** and **Reit im Winkel**. These three health resorts are connected by an Alpine road, that passes by small lakes and protected scenic areas. The place which is best-known for winter sports is Reit im Winkel, whose fame in this category dates much farther back than the Olympic enterprises of *Gold-Rosi* Mittermaier from the Winklmoosalm in 1976. Inzell is a renowned skating center, while Ruhpolding becomes a Mecca in summer for fans of other types of local sports – wrestling, *Fingerhakln* and *Strängkatznziagn* for self-achievement by participants and the enjoyment of the public.

La región de Chiemgau

Como el Berchtesgaden, también el Chiemgau hace parte de aquellos distritos del Alta Baviera que fueron integrados en el Reino de Baviera solamente a principios del siglo décimonono.

Antes, la región que circunda el mayor lago de Baviera quedaba bajo la influencia política, religiosa y cultural del Obispado de Salisburgo y de sus conventos. A la situacion económica del Chiemgau contribuyó, además de la agricultura, sobre todo el transporte de la sal de Bad Reichenhall, antes que se descubrise que el Chiemsee y las Chiemgauer Alpen podían ser aprovechados como loca-lidades veraniegas de reposo.

El *Bayerisches Meer*, de 84,5 quilómetros cuadrados, debe su popularidad, no solo a su óptima posición en los empalmes este-oeste entre Salisburgo y Munich, a las condiciones ideales para los deportes de agua y al clima apacible durante el invierno y en las noches de verano, el lago actua como acumulador térmico – mas también a algunas famosas curiosidades ubicadas sobre y en el lago: desde la estación termal de Prien para la cura de Kneipp, la *chiemsee-bâhnle* conduce al puerto, de donde los barcos conducen los visitantes a las dos grandes islas, que dan su nombre a los dos claustros de **Frauenworth** y de **Herrenworth**. Mas, mientras el claustro de las monjas, todavía subsiste en la *Fraueninsel* – la Gasthaus del claustro y el licor que allí se ofrece son famosos – la *Herreninsel* propone una atracción muy diferente: el **Neues Schloss** una reconstrucción del Castillo de Versailles, cuya construcción tuvo inicio bajo Ludwig II en 1878. El monumento dedicado a Luis XIV de Borbón y las ideas sobre el absolutismo no fueron nunca realizadas y el mismo soberano no usó nunca su cama de lujo en el *cuarto de dormir de parada*, pero, los más de 600.000 turistas que cada año visitan el Castillo consiguen, de cualquier modo, hacerse una idea del mundo imaginario de Ludwig.

Menos espectacular, pero en compensación más tranquilo, es el **hinterland** del Chiemsee – por ejemplo los laguillos como el Klostersee con el claústro de **Seeon**, el castillo de Hohenaschau a los pies de la **Kampenwand** o el triángulo de Chiemgau entre Inzell, **Ruhpolding** y **Reit** im Winkel. Estas tres estaciones climáticas son ligadas por una carretera alpina, que pasa a lo largo de pequeños lagos y zonas panorámicas protegidas. La localidad de mayor atracción para los deportes invernales es Reit im Winkel, y no solamente de las empresas olímpicas de *Gold-Rosi* Mittermaier sobre el Winkmoosalm, en 1976. Inzell es un centro muy famoso para patinar, mientras en Ruhpolding, durante el verano, también son practicados otros tipos de deportes *regionales*.

Photo at top: View from Mt. Kampenwand over the Chiemsee with Fraueninsel (Ladies' Island) and Herreninsel (Men's Island)
Large photo at bottom: Seeon monastery near the Chiemsee, north of Seebruck
Small photo 1: Chiemsee railway
Small photo 2: Procession in costume at Prien am Chiemsee

Figura arriba: Panorama desde Kampenwand sobre Chiemsee con la Isla de la Señoras y la Isla de los Señores.
Figura grande abajo: Convento de Seeon en las cercanías del Chiemsee, al norte de Seebruck.
Figura pequeña 1: Tren del Chiemsee.
Figura pequeña 2: Desfile de disfraces en Prien am Chiemsee.

1

2

Page 28, top photo: Evening atmosphere on the Chiemsee
Page 28, bottom photo: Gstadt: steamer landing stage, with Fraueninsel in the background and the Chiemgau mountains behind
Page 29, top photo: View from Gstadt over Fraueninsel
Page 29, bottom photo: Carolingian Portal on Fraueninsel

Página 28 arriba: Atmósfera nocturna en Chiemsee.
Página 28 abajo: Gstadt - Atracadero con la Isla de las Señoras al fondo, y las montañas del Chiemgau.
Página 29 arriba: Vista de Gstadt en la Isla de las Señoras.
Página 29 abajo: Portal Carolíngio en la Isla de las Señoras.

Plate 1: **Herrenchiemsee Castle, an imitation of Versailles**
Plate 2: **Herrenchiemsee Castle gardens**
Plate 3: **Detail of Mirror Room (portrait of King Ludwig II)**
Plate 4: **Holy Rood Chapel on the Herrenchiemsee**
Plate 5: **Paddle steamer on the Chiemsee**
Plate 6: **The famous Mirror Room in Herrenchiemsee Castle**

Figura 1: Castillo de Herrenchiemsee, imitación de Versailles.
Figura 2: Los jardines del Castillo de Herrenchiemsee.
Figura 3: Detalle de la sala de los espejos (retrato de Ludwig II)
Figura 4: Capilla de Santa Cruz en Herrenchiemsee.
Figura 5: Piróscafo de ruedas en Chiemsee.
Figura 6: La famosa sala de los espejos en el Castillo de Herrenchiemsee.

5

6

Large photo: Frillensee looking towards Mt. Hochstaufen (1771 m)
Small photos:
Plate 1: Inzell: St. Nicholas' hermitage
Plate 2: Inzell: St. Michael's Parish Church
Plate 3: Mt. Rauschberg (1671 m): jumping-off point for hang-gliders
Plate 4: Rauschberg cableway
Large photo, p. 33: Ruhpolding

Figura grande: Frillensee hacia Hochstaufen (1771 m.).
Figuras pequeñas:
Figura 1: Inzell: Iglesia de eremitorio de San Nicola.
Figura 2: Inzell: parroquia de San Michael.
Figura 3: Rauschberg (1671 m.) - salida de los deltaplanos.
Figura 4: Teleferica de Rauschberg.
Figura grande, página 33: Ruhpolding.

Large photo: Reit im Winkl
Plate 1: Sleigh-ride in the neighbourhood of Reit im Winkl
Plate 2: Feeding the game near Reit im Winkl
Plate 3: Reit im Winkl, St. Pancras Parish Church
Plate 4: "Winklmoosalm" Chapel

Figura grande: Reit im Winkl.
Figura 1: Excursión en trineo en las cercanías de Reit im Winkl.
Figura 2: Forrajear de la caza en Reit im Winkl.
Figura 3: Reit im Winkl; Parroquia de San Pancracio.
Figura 4: Capilla sobre el "Winklmoosalm"

4

The Tegernsee region

La región de Tegernsee

The Tegernsee region owes its early development as a tourist-spot to the Bavarian king, Max I. Joseph who, at the beginning of the nineteenth century, transformed the abandoned Benedictine monastery on the lake into a summer castle called the Sommerschloss. Although, in the meantime, wide roads running along the shores and the four leading localities – **Tegernsee, Rottach-Egern, Gmund** and **Bad Wiessee**, with its famous thermoiodic and sulphuric springs – continue to get bigger and bigger, the Tegernsee region still has a great deal to offer in the way of beautiful spots. One of the most beautiful views is that of the Wallberg (1,722 meters), which can be reached by cable car from Rottach-Egern. From there the eye can not only sweep over the entire Tegernsee territory but also see as far as the Grossglockner, the Zugspitze and even Munich. The north wing of **Tegernsee Schloss** houses the *Ducal factory of Bavarian Beer* which has its own beer-house.

From Rottach-Egern, a small toll-road takes you to the skiing area of Spitzingsee, located 1,800 metres up, and the health resort of Schliersee. Not far from here in the Leitzachtal, which lies behind this area, there is a mountain village, Bayrischzell, snuggled at the foot of the Wendelstein (1,838 m).

The ski slopes on the Wendelstein do not have to be reached only from Bayrischzell (by cable car) but can be approached from Brannenburg im Inntal, also. From here, a rack railway built in 1912, the oldest mountain railway in Bavaria, carries you for a distance of 10 kilometers through several tunnels to the Wendelstein-haus. Another spot skiers love is **Sudelfeld**, at the end of the Leitzachtal. Once here, you find yourself not far from the *Feuriger Tatzelwurm* inn, which owes its name to a chronically parched dragon that used to slake its thirst at the Aurbach Falls nearby.

La región del Tegersee debe su prematura explotación turística al rey bávaro Max I Joseph, que, a principios del siglo décimonono transformó el abandonado claustro benedictino ubicado en la ribera del lago en un castillo para el verano, el Sommerschloss.

En el intermedio grandes carreteras corren a lo largo de las riberas y las cuatros principales localidades – **Tegernsee, Rottach-Egern, Gmund** y **Bad Wiessee,** con las famosas fuentes termo-yódicas y sulfúreas – continuan a crecer, la región del Tegernsee ofrece aún bellas localidades. Una de las más encantadoras vistas es aquella del Wallberg (711 m), que puede ser alcanzada de Rottach-Egern por medio de funicular aéreo.

El **Schloss de Tegernsee** por otra parte ofrece no solo placeres culturales, mas también concretamente físicos: en el ala norte se encuentra la *Ducal fábrica de cerveza bávara* con una pequeña cervecería.

Desde Rottach-Egern, una pequeña calle con peaje lleva a la localidad para esquiar de Spitzingsee ubicada a 1800 m. y a la estación climática de Schliersee. No lejos de aquí, en la Leitzachtal que se queda detrás, encuéntrase un pueblo de montaña, Bayrischzell, a los pies del Wendelstein (1838 m).

La localidad para esquiar puesta en el Wendelstein no es alcanzable solamente de Bayrischzell (con el funicular aéreo) mas también de Brannenburg im Inntal: de aquí, un ferrocarril de cremallera construido en 1912, el más viejo ferrocarril de montaña de la Baviera, lleva por 10 quilómetros, atravesando numerosos túneles, a Wendelsteinhaus. Otra localidad predilecta para esquiar es **Sudelfeld**, a fines de la Leitzachtal. Aquí, no estamos muy lejos de la Gasthof *Feuriger Tatzelwurm,* que debe su nombre a la leyenda de un dragón que un tiempo tenía la costumbre de quitarse la sed en las vicinas caídas de Auerbach.

Page 37: Rottach-Egern, painters' corner "Malerwinkel"

Página 37: Rottach-Egern, ángulo des pintores "Malerwinkel"

Large photo: view of the Tegernsee showing Tegernsee, the villages of Rottach-Egern and Bad Wiessee. Mt. Wallberg can be seen in the background
Plate 1: Bad Wiessee
Plate 2: Folk festival on the Tegernsee
Plate 3: A lakeside walk at Bad Wiessee

Figura grande: Vista sobre Tegernsee y las localidades de Rottach-Egern y Bad Wiessee, atrás, el Wallberg.
Figura 1: Bad Wiesee.
Figura 2: Fiesta folklórica en el Tegernsee
Figura 3: Paseo sobre la orilla en Bad Wiesee.

Small photo at bottom: Bayrischzell
Photo on right: Mt. Wendelstein with the rack railway and Wendelstein church (the highest church in Germany)
Large photo at bottom: The Spitzingsee
Small photo, p. 41: Costume festival at Schliersee
Large photo, p. 41: Schliersee village

Figura pequeña abajo: Bayrischzell.
Figura a la derecha: El Wendelstein con el ferrocarril de cremallera e iglesia de Wendelstein (la iglesia más alta de Alemania).
Figura grande abajo: El Spitzingsee.
Figura pequeña, p. 41: Fiesta en trajes en Schliersee.
Figura grande: El pueblo de Schliersee

Isarwinkel-Tölz region

Isarwinkel is that region which stretches along the upper segment of the Isar, between Vorderriss and Bad Tölz, where the river flows out of the large Alpine valley to empty into the Bavarian plain. **Bad Tölz** is divided in half by the Isar. On the right bank is the Old Town with its lean-to-roofed houses painted in vivid colours. On the left bank is the spa with its healing baths and hotels, located near thermoiodic springs, whose waters may be used for either drinking or immersion. In addition to the Old Town there is the **Kalvarienberg** with a church to which pilgrimages are made and where, each year, during the traditional *Leonhardifahrt*, horses are blessed.

Wolfratshausen is an old town on rafts, from which, once upon a time, beer, furniture and wood were shipped to Munich; one of the current tourist attractions consists, in fact, of rides on rafts down the Isar River to the Valley.

The upper segment of the Isar represents another important economic resource, as it supplies energy to hydroelectric plants. Near the Austrian Border, at the edge of a natural park in the Karwendelgebirge, we find the Sylvenstein basin, for whose construction a amall village had to be sacrificed in 1959.

Part of the water of the Isar is taken, by means of a conduit in the rock, to the biggest hydroelectric plant in Upper Bavaria between **Walchensee** and **Kochelsee.**

From the **Herzogstand** (1,731 m) the two lakes can be seen. At Kochel, there is a monument dedicated to the ironworker Balthes, a native of Kochel who, in 1705, at the head of a group of farm-workers, took part in the struggle for the liberation of Munich from Austrian domination and was killed in the Battle of Sendlingen.

Other noted spas include **Kreuth**, between the Isar and the Tegernsee, and **Lenggries**, situated halfway between the Sylvensteinsee and Bad Tölz on the Isar.

La Isarwinkel y la región de Tölz

La *Isarwinkel* es aquella región que se extiende a lo largo del curso superior del Isar, entre Vorderriss y Bad Tölz, en donde el río, saliendo del valle alpino, entra en la planície bávara.

Bad Tölz es dividida por el Isar en dos mitades: en la ribera derecha hállase la ciudad vieja con sus casas con los techos de faldas, pintadas de colores vivos, en la ribera izquierda, encuéntrase el barrio termal, con los establecimientos de cura y los hoteles, situados en las proximidades de las fuentes termoyódicas, cuyas aguas pueden ser utilizadas para beber o para inmersiones. Además de la ciudad vieja, hay el Kalvarienberg con una iglesia que es objeto de peregrinajes y en donde cada año, por la ocasión del tradicional *Leonhardifahrt,* son benedecidos los caballos.

Wolfratshausen es una vieja ciudad sobre gabarras, de donde un tiempo, cerveza, muebles y maderaje eran transportados para Munich. Una de las atracciones turísticas de nuestros días trae origen precisamente de viajes sobre gabarras a lo largo del Isar, hacia valle.

El curso superior del Isar representa más una y muy importante fuente económica, ya que suministra la energía a las centrales hidroeléctricas. En las proximidades de la frontera austríaca, cerca del parque natural de Karwendelgebirge, es ubicada la cuenca de Sylvenstein, por cuya construcción fue sacrificado, en el año de 1959, el viejo castillo del cual, en los períodos de bajío, aún es posible ver lo que queda de los muros bajo el grande puente.

Una parte del agua del Isar es encaminada, al través de un conducto de piedras, a la grande central hidroeléctrica del Alta Baviera entre Walchensee y Kochelsee.

Desde el Herzogstand (1731 m) se pueden ver los dos lagos. En Kochel, hay un monumento dedicado al herrero Balthes, de Kochel, que, en el año de 1705, al frente de los campesinos tomó parte a la lucha para la liberación de Munich del dominio austríaco, y murió durante la batalla de Sendlingen.

Célebres estaciones termales son también las de Kreuth, entre el Isar y el Tegernsee, y Lenggries, ubicadas a mitad del camino entre Silvensteinsee y Bad Tölz sobre el Isar.

Photo on right: Wackersberg near Bad Tölz
P. 43 top photo: Silvenstein reservoir
P. 43 bottom photo: Lenggries

Figura a la derecha: Wackersberg cerca de Bad Tölz.
Figura p. 43 arriba: Lago artificial de Silvenstein.
Figura p. 43 abajo: Lenggries.

Large photo: Bad Tölz: the historic Marktstrasse (Market Street)
Plate 1: Interior of Kalvarienberg Church
Plate 2: Spa
Plate 3: View over the Isar towards Mt. Kalvarienberg with the Sanctuary
Plate 4: St. Leonard's procession on Mt. Kalvarienberg

Figura grande: Bad Tölz - la histórica Carretera del Mercado.
Figura 1: Interior de la iglesia del Kalvarienberg.
Figura 2: Centro termal
Figura 3: Vista sobre Isar hacia el Kalvarienberg con el Santuario.
Figura 4: La procesión de San Leonardo sobre el Kalvarienberg.

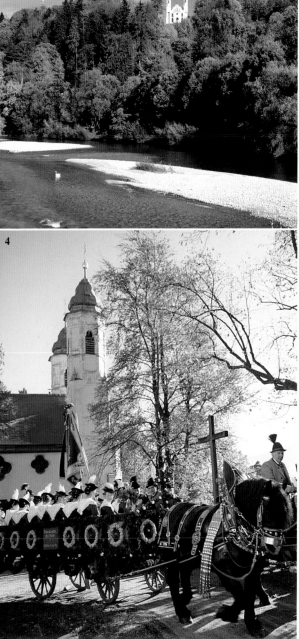

Large photo: Herzogstand cableway with view of the Walchensee
Plate 1: Kochelsee with Triminibad looking towards Mt. Herzogstand
Plate 2: Kochel, small church looking towards Mt. Herzogstand
Plate 3: The Walchensee looking towards Jochberg
Plate 4: Walchensee hydroelectric station
Plate 5: Surfing on the Walchensee
Plate 6: Kochel am See with the smith of Kochel memorial, and Hotel Zur Post

Figura grande: Teleférico de Herzogstand con vistas sobre el lago Walchen.
Figura 1: Kochelsee con Triminibad hacia la cima de Herzogstand.
Figura 2: Kochel, pequeña iglesia sobre Herzogstand.
Figura 3: Walchensee hacia Jochberg.
Figura 4: Central eléctrica de Walchensee.
Figura 5: Surf sobre Walchensee.
Figura 6: Kochel am See: el monumento de Kochel y el Hotel Zur Post.

The Werdenfels

The most famous tourist region in Upper Bavaria is located at the foot of the Zugspitze. It is the Werdenfelserland around Garmisch-Partenkirchen. The area gets its name from a medieval castle, whose nickname was *land of gold*, during the period of its economic boom, between the fourteenth and seventeenth centuries, when **Mittenwald and Partenkirchen** used it as an intermediate trading stage between northern Italy and Augsburg and Nuremberg. Mittenwald was one of the first small towns to make a comeback from the consequences of the Thirty Years' War, thanks to a violin-maker by the name of Mathias Klotz who founded, in the seventeenth century, the local stringed instrument industry, which is still thriving on the local market of Upper Isar, rounded out by a school for apprentices and a violin museum.

In the nineteenth century the discovery by the inhabitants of the big cities of the natural beauties of Garmisch gave the latter an enormous economic boost. Then, when the construction of the railway Munich-Garmisch was completed (1889), well-to-do burghers repaired to **Garmisch** and **Partenkirchen** to take the cure at the thermoiodic and sulphur springs and relax in the comfort of the hotels. Houses and villas for vacationers went up everywhere, and the two sites kept growing along the same lines until they are united into one, single community.

In the twentieth century, the transformation of Garmisch-Partenkirchen into a world-famous tourist center was closely tied to a burgeoning interest in winter sports. In 1905 the first ski club had already been founded in Partenkirchen, the first ski-jumps appeared on the Kochelberg, the first bobsled run was built in 1911 beside the Riessersee, and, in the twenties, the Wank and Kreuzeck ski runs were made accessible by cable car followed, finally, by those on the Zugspitze. For the 1936 Olympic Games, ice and ski stadiums were added.

An experience which should not be missed is a trip on the Zugspitze railroad in the Wettersteingebirge. This railway, built in 1930, leaves the station at Garmisch-Partenkirchen, passes the Riessersee and Grainau at the foot of the awe-inspiring Waxenstein and chugs on to the shadowy Eibsee, surrounded by woods, which was formed by the collapse of a mountain in the glacial epoch. From here, the rack railway starts its climb, passing through the Riffelriss woods on the majestic northern side of the Zugspitze and then, winding up a double curve, comes to the Schneeferner Alpine hut, ensconced at a height of 2,650 meters. By using a cable car, you can reach the highest mountain peak in West Germany (2,964 m). On foot, it is possible to get to the Zugspitze by passing throung the **Partnach** Gorge beyond the Knorrhütte to the Schneeferner, or by going directly through the Höllental, until you get to the Gipfelkreuz.

Garmisch-Partenkirchen is, therefore, the center of the Werdenfelser region, but it should be remembered that the many possibilities offered there are not limited to the region at the bottom of the Zugspitze. The **Krün** and **Wallgau** spas on the road to the Walchensee are part, also, of the *land of gold*, as well as the areas along the Loisach, between Garmisch and **Murnau**, where the **Staffelsee** with its seven islands and healing, marshy water brings large numbers of guests to its shores every year. A few kilometers to the east of Murnau, there is an open-air museum in **Glentleitn** which has roughly a dozen old farmhouses in addition to numerous artisans' houses and ateliers, where the wood-carving craftsmanship tradition has been kept

alive. To the west of the marshy Murnau zone lies the mud-spa, **Bad Kohlgrub**.

Those who return to Garmisch along the Ammer pass by **Oberammergau**, a place which is known only as a summer resort and wood-carving center for nine years. Then, every tenth year, it becomes the talk of every town in the world because of its Passion Play, which is put on every ten years following a vow made during the Plague of 1633. The next performance is due in 2000. Until then, visitors will have to be satisfied with other items of interest such as the figures sculpted by wood-carvers of sacred images, the houses with their fascinating frescoes and the magnificent rococo church.

The builder of the Oberammergau Church, Joseph Schmuzer, created many fine works in that region, for instance at Ettal, in the Benedectine Cloister, visited by many people also because of the famous liquor made by the Friars.

Once in Ettal, it doesn't take long to get to the Valley of the Ammer where, in the natural park of its mountains, is situated one of those castles which infuriated the Government of the then king, Ludwig II, but which made him immortal in the eyes of future generations, **Schloss Linderhof**.

This structure, done in a lavish rococo style, surrounded by lush gardens with falls, fountains, the Temple of Venus, a grotto and a Moorish temple, is a tribute to both absolute monarchy and the theatrical world of Richard Wagner.

Astounding, by the way, is the use made, at Linderhof, of technologies which were highly sophisticated for that era and which made possible unusual strategems such as the raising of a table set for dinner from the ground floor to the dining-room.

The lighting of the castle was provided by an electric plant, one of the first in Bavaria. And, in the Venusgrotte a subterranean motor generated lapping wave movements.

At "Gschwandtnerbauer" with the Zugspitze chain (from left to right: Alpspitze, Zugspitze and Waxensteine) near Garmisch-Partenkirchen

Figura p. 49: En "Gschwandtnerbauer" y al fondo, de izquierda a derecha las cimas: Alpspitze, Zugspitze, Waxensteine en Garmisch - Partenkirchen.

La región de Werdenfels

La región turística más renombrada del Alta Baviera es ubicada a los pies del Zugspitze: es la Werdenfeserland alrededor de Garmisch-Partenkirchen. La localidad asume el nombre de un castillo medioeval, cuyo sobrenombre *tierra de oro* débese al período de su floración económica, entre el siglo décimocuarto y el siglo décimoséptimo, cuando **Mittenwald** y **Partenkirchen** la utilizaban como etapa intermedia del comercio entre el norte de Italia y Augusta y Nuremberg. Mittenwald fue una de las primeras ciudades que se han recobrado de las consecuencias de la guerra de los trinta años, gracias a un constructor de violines, mathias Klotz, que en el siglo décimoséptimo, fundó la industria local de los instrumentos de cuerdas.

En el siglo décimonono, el descubrimiento, por los habitantes de la ciudad, de las bellezas naturales de Garmisch, dió a esta última un grande lanzamiento económico. Cuando, después, fue completada la construcción del ferrocarril Munich-Garmisch (1889), la burguesía acaudalada trasladábase a **Garmisch y a Partenkirchen** para curarse en las fuentes termoyódicas y sulfúreas y para lajarse en los hoteles llenos de comodidades. Casas y villas para veraneantes surgieron por doquiera y ambas las localidades deserrolláranse paralelamente, e constituyendo en 1935 una única comunidad.

En el siglo veinte, la transformación de Garmisch-Partenkirchen en un centro turístico de fama mundial es estrechamente ligada a la *escalation* de los deportes invernales: ya en 1905, en Partenkirchen fue fundado el primero Club para esquiadores, en el Kochelberg surgieron los primeros trampolines, junto al Riessersee fue construída, en 1911, la primera pista de bob y, en los años veinte, fueron volvidos accesibles, mediante funiculares aéreos, los campos de esquí del Wank y del Krenzeck y, por último, también aquellos del Zugspitze. Para los juegos olímpicos, de 1936, fueron añadidos un estadio del hielo y uno de esquí.

Una de las experiencias que, en ningún caso, deberá esquivar en los Wettersteingebirge es un viaje con el ferrocarril del Zugspitze: desde la estación de Garmisch-Partenkirchen, dicho ferrocarril, construído en 1930, lleva, al través de las estaciones de Riesserstee y Grainau a los pies del imponente Waxenstein, hasta el sombrio Eibsee, circundado por bosques, que se ha formado en consecuencia del derrumbamiento de una montaña en el era glacial. Desde aquí el ferrocarril de cremallera sube, atravéss del bosque, al Riffelriss de la majestuosa pared norte del Zugspitze y luego, con una curva doble, hasta la cabaña alpina de Schreeferner, a una altura de 2650 metros. Luego con una funicular aérea es posible alcanzar la cumbre más alta de Alemania Federal (2964 m). A pie se alcanza el Zugspitze pasando por la garganta de Partnach más allá de la Knorrhütte hasta Schneeferner, o al través de la Hollental directamente hasta Gipfelkreuz.

Garmisch-Partenkirchen es, por lo tanto, el centro de la región de Werdenfelser, pero las muchas posibilidades que la región les ofrece no se limitan solo al Zugspitze: también las estaciones termales de **Krûn** y de **Wallgau** que se encuentran en la carretera que se dirige al Walchensee hacen parte de la **tierra de oro,** así como las localidades a lo largo del Loisach, entre Garmisch y **Murnau**, en donde el **Staffelsee** con sus siete islas y su àgua palustre con propiedades curativas atrae numerosos huéspedes. Pocos quilómetros a este de Murnau, encuéntrase la pequeña ciudad-museo de **Glentleiten** con aproximadamente 200 viejas masadas, numerosas casas y laboratorios de artesanía, en los cuales se mantiene viva la tradición del trabajo artesano de la madera. A oeste de la zona pantanosa de Murnau, se encuentra **Bad Kohlgrub**, la estación de fangos termales más alta de la República de Alemania.

Quien desde Bad Kohlgrub, a lo largo del Ammer, vuelve a Garmisch, pasa a través de **Oberammergau**, localidad que por nueve años es renombrada exclusivamente como localidad de veraneo y de trabajo de la madera, mientras cada décimo año es al centro del interés por su Misterio de la Pasión, que es puesta en escena de diez en diez años, por un ex voto hecho durante la epidemia de peste de 1633. La próxima edición se desarrollará en 2000. hasta entonces, los visitantes deberán contentarse con otras curiosidades: las figuras de madera del entallador de imágenes sagradas, las casas embellecidas con frescos o la maravillosa iglesia rococó.

El constructor de la iglesia de Oberammergau, Joseph Schmuzer; dejó vestigios de su obra también en la vicina Ettal, en la iglesia del claustro benedictino que muchos huéspedes visitan también por el licor que allí es destilado.

A quien llegó a Ettal, no le queda mucho para alcanzar la valle del Ammer, en donde, en el parque natural de sus montes, surge uno de aquellos castillos que enajenaron del Gobierno de entonces Ludwig II, mas volvieron inmortal a las futuras generaciones, Schloss Linderhof. Dicha construcción, de un exuberante estilo rococó, circundada por espléndidos jardines con caídas, fontanas, el Tempio de Venus, una gruta y un templo morisco, es al mismo tiempo un homenaje a la monarquía absoluta y al mundo teatral de Wagner, venerado y ayudado por Ludwig.

Entre otras cosas, aturde el hecho que en Linderhof se haya recurrido a tecnologías muy sofisticadas para el época, que permitían extraños engaños, cuales el solevantamiento de la mesa puesta del soberano desde la planta baja hasta el comedor.

A la iluminación del castillo proveía una especial central eléctrica, una de las primeras construídas en Baviera y en la Venusgrotte un motor subterráneo encargábase del movimiento de las olas.

Large photo: Garmisch-Partenkirchen in winter, with Mt. Alpspitze (2628 m)
Small plate 1: Hochalm cableway looking towards Garmisch-Partenkirchen
Plate 2: Zugspitzplatt with Sonn-Alpin
Plate 3: New Year ski-jumping at Garmisch-Partenkirchen

Figura grande: Garmisch - Partenkirchen en invierno con las cimas de Alpspitze (2628 m.).
Figura pequeña 1: Funicular de Hochalm hacia Garmisch - Partenkirchen.
Figura 2: Zugspitzplatt con Sonn - Alpin.
Figura 3: Garmisch-Partenkirchen: Salto en ski el día de Año Nuevo.

1

2

3

Large photo on p. 52: Riessersee with Kleiner and Grosser Waxenstein
Small photo on p. 52: Wamberg (996 m), the highest village in Germany
Top: View from Mt. Wank towards Garmisch-Partenkirchen and the Zugspitze chain
Bottom: Frühlingstrasse in Garmisch

Figura grande p. 52: Rießersee con Kleiner y Großer Waxenstein.
Figura pequeña p. 52: Wamberg (996 m.), el pueblecito más alto de Alemania.
Arriba: Vista del Wank sobre Garmisch - Partenkirchen y la cima del Zugspitze.
Abajo: la Frühlingstraße en Garmisch.

Small photo: Eibsee with pleasure boat, looking towards the Zugspitze
Large photo: Grainau village with Catholic parish church, Grosser and Kleiner Waxenstein in the background.

Figura pequeña: Eibsee: vuelta enbarca con vistas de Zugspitze.
Figura grande: Pueblecito Grainau con una parroquia católica, detrás el Großer y el Kleiner Waxenstein.

Station on summit with Münchnerhaus and glacier cableway to Mt. Sonn-Alpin.

Estación en la cima, con Münchnerhaus y el funicular sobre el ventisquero que va hacia Sonn - Alpin.

View of Mt. Zugspitze with cross on summit (2964 m), looking towards the Austrian Alps

Panorama sobre Zugspitze con una cruz en la cima (2964 m.) hacia los Alpes austriacos.

Mittenwald-Krün-Wallgau

Large photo: The Lautersee looking towards the Wetterstein mountains
Plate 1: Violin maker's workshop in Mittenwald
Plate 2: Mittenwald with Karwendelgebirge (2476 m)
Plate 3: Karwendel cableway, mountain station
Plate 4: Obermarkt in Mittenwald with the Parish Church of SS. Peter and Paul
Plate 5: Krün, looking towards Karwendel mountains
Plate 6: Wallgau (mural)

Figura grande: El Lautersee hacia Wettersteingebirge.
Figura 1: Laboratorio para la producción de violines en Mittenwald.
Figura 2: Mittenwald con Karwendelgebirge (2476 m.).
Figura 3: Funicular del Karwendel. Estación de montaña.
Figura 4: Obermarkt a Mittenwald con la parroquia de los Santos Pedro y Pablo.
Figura 5: Krün hacia Karwendelgebirge.
Figura 6: Wallgau (murales).

Ettal monastery

Ettal Benedictine monastery, built in 1330 by Kaiser Ludwig the Bavarian, was destroyed by fire in 1733 and subsequently rebuilt in Rococo style by Josef Schmutzer. The central feature is the basilica, with its 59 metre high cupola, and the huge frescoes.

La Abadía benedictina de Ettal, construida en 1330 por el Emperador Ludovico el Bávaro, fue destruida en 1733 por un incendio y reconstruida, en los años sucesivos, en estilo rococó por Josef Schmutzer. El núcleo está constituido por una basílica con una cúpula de 59 m. de altura y frescos gigantescos.

Linderhof

Among the most famous of Ludwig II's castles is Schloss Linderhof, built between 1874 and 1878, a luxurious Rococo residence in Louis XIV style. Linderhof is the only castle in which King Ludwig II lived for any lenght of time.

De entre los castillos más famosos de Ludwig II, figura el Castillo de Linderhof construido entre 1874 y 1878, una lujosa construcción de estilo rococó, imitando la residencia de Luis XIV. Linderhof es el único castillo en el cual el Rey Ludwig II vivió durante mucho tiempo.

Plate 1: Schloss Linderhof with gardens
Plate 2: The Moorish pavilion
Plate 3: The dining room, with adjustable table
Plate 4: The Blue Grotto
Plate 5: The bedroom

Figura 1: El castillo de Linderhof con los jardines.
Figura 2: El quiosco moresco.
Figura 3: El comedor con una mesa regulable en su altura.
Figura 4: La gruta azul.
Figura 5: El dormitorio.

Oberammergau
Page 62, large photo: Oberammergau, looking towards Mt. Kofel (1342 m)
Small photos: Religious plays in Oberammergau
Bottom right: Little Red Riding Hood's house

Photos on page 63
Plate 1: Bad Kohlgrub
Plate 2: Pfaffenwinkel nature reserve, Altenauer Moor, Tiefsee
Plate 3: Murnauer Moos
Plate 4: Staffelsee near Murnau
Plate 5: Murnau

Página 62, figura grande: Oberammergau hacia el Kofel (1342 m.).
Figuras pequeña: Representaciones sacras en Oberammergau
Figura abajo a la derecha: la casa de Caperucita Roja.

Figuras Página 63:
Figura 1: Bad Kohlgrub.
Figura 2: Parque natural de Pfaffenwinkel, Altenauer Moor, Tiefsee.
Figura 3: Murnauer Moos.
Figura 4: Staffelsee en Murnau.
Figura 5: Murnau.

Freilichtmuseum Glentleiten

Plate 1: Weissenbachgütlhaus from Rottau, view of the Kochelsee with Schlehdorf Monastery
Plates 2 and 3: Part of the open-air Museum - Glentleiten
Plate 4: Loisach-Floss, with wooden chapel and farmhouses in the background

Figura 1: Weißenbachgütlhaus Rottau, vista desde el Kochelsee con el Convento de Schlehdorf.
Figuras 2 y 3: En el Museo - Glentleiten
Figura 4: Loisach- Floß con capilla de madera y las casas de los campesinos al fondo.

Page 65
Left: Rottenbuch with the Zugspitze (2964 m)
Bottom: Rottenbuch Monastery church
Figura a la izquierda: Rottenbuch con la Zugspitze (2964 m)
Figura abajo: Iglesia del Convento de Rottenbuch.

Pfaffenwinkel

To the north of the region of Werdenfels, between the Lech, the Ammer and the Loisach, the expanse of the Pfaffenwinkel is to be found, which takes its name from numerous baroque and rococo churches and cloisters in the area.

Two of the most interesting structures in the area are, for example, the **Rottenbuch** Cloister, with its parochial church and, above all, the Wieskirche, whose interior, done by Dominikus Zimmermann (1685-1766), is a rococo masterpiece.

Not far from the Wieskirche, between Rottenbuch and **Bayersoien**, there is an area which anyone who loves streams will like. Most visitors prefer to limit themselves, however, to looking down at the devastating whirlpool of the Ammer from a height of 76 meters on the **Echelsbach Bridge** at the point where the river branches off in the direction of **Steingaden.**

◆

Al norte de la región de Werdenfelser, entre el Lech, el Ammer y el Loisach, se extiende el *Pfaffenwinkel,* que toma el nombre de numerosas iglesias y claustros barrocos y rococó presentes en la localidad.

Entre las construcciones de mayor interés de la localidad podemos mencionar, como ejemplo, el claustro de Rottebuch, con su iglesia parroquial, y especialmente la Wieskirche, cuyo interior, obra de Dominikus Zimmermann (1685-1766) es una de las obras maestras del rococó.

No lejos de Wieskirche, entre Rottenbuch y Bayersoien, hay una localidad que llenará de placer los que aman los torrentes.

Mas la mayoría de los visitantes profieren limitarse a observar desde lo alto el abismo trastornador del Ammer – desde los 76 metros de altura del Puente de Echelsbach en la bifurcación hacia Steingaden.

Wieskirche

At Hochmoor (Moor) near Steingaden stands one of the jewels of Pfaffenwinkel: the Rococo church built by Dominikus Zimmermann between 1745 and 1753. The magnificent interiors with the slender double pillars and delicate ceiling frescoes produce the effect of celestial halls.

◆

En la Hochmoor en Steingaden se encuentra la iglesia rococó construida por Dominikus Zimmermann 1745-1753, una joya de Pfaffenwinkel. Los suntuosos interiores con los altos pilastres dobles y los delicados frescos que decoran el techo dan la sensación de una sala celeste.

The Royal Castles at Füssen

Los Castillos reales de Füssen

Strictly speaking, the region to the east of Füssen, even though located this side of Lech, is part of the district of Schwaben. However, there is so much that is worthwhile seeing, that a brief detour for travellers to Upper Bavaria is justified. The most famous structure on the Austro-German border no longer needs any introduction. In fact, in 1985, the year before the centennial of the death of Ludwig II provided an occasion for the influx of millions of visitors from all over the world to **Neuschwanstein** Castle. It was here, in this fantastic retreat, that the Bavarian sovereign took refuge in June, 1886, when he was removed from the throne because of mental illness – the first time in history this has ever happened – and confined to the Starnbergersee. As Ludwig wrote to Wagner, whose operas inspired him to build Neuschwanstein, he had observed from the nearby castle of **Hohenschwangau** the construction of the *Märchenschloss* in *pure feudal castle style.* Hohenschwangau on the Alpsee had already been built in 1832 by Ludwig's father, Max II. As opposed to his pacifist son, Max II had used the place as a hunting preserve. He wanted, for example, to have a hunting lodge built on the Tegelberg, from which he could enjoy a view of the Alps of Ammergau, Lech and the Füssen lake region.

The largest of the lakes, today a spot preferred by water sports enthusiasts, could not have been foreseen by the King of Bavaria in the nineteenth century. It is the **Forggensee**, which was formed by the damming up of the Lech for an electric power plant. Its basin extends almost as far as Füssen, the old town on the edge of the Lechtal. It lies in the shadow of the **Hohes Schloss**, the oldest castle in the region. It was built in the thirteenth century and was used as a summer residence by prince-bishops. It now has a collection of paintings as well as the Magistrate's Court.

En sentido estricto, también la región que se encuentra a este de Füssen, mismo siendo ubicada a este lado del Lech, ya hace parte del districto de Schwaben.

Mas las maravillas de tal localidad justifican una pequeña desviación para quien viaja en Baviera. La más renombrada construcción, puesta al confin austro-germánico ya no necessita de presentación y, ya en el año de 1985, en el centenario de la muerte de Ludwig II, allí llegaron millones de visitantes de todos los Paises: es el **Castillo de Neuschwanstein**. En esta fantástica construcción, el soberano bávaro halló refugio en el mes de junio de 1886, cuando, único caso en la historia, fue destituído del trono por su enfermedad mental y fue confinado en el Starnbergsee. Como Ludwig tuvo ocasión de escribir a Wagner, de cuyas obras había traído inspiración también para llevar a cabo la construcción de Neuschwanstein, él observara desde el vicino castillo de **Hohenschwangau** la construcción del *Märchenschloss* en *puro estilo de los castillos feudales.*

Hohenschwangau junto al Alpsee fuera construído ya en el año de 1832 por el padre de Ludwig, Max II.

A diferencia del hijo pacifista, Max II había explotado la localidad como reserva de caza, a Tegelberg, desde el cual se gozaba la vista de los Alpes de Ammergau, del Lech y de la región lacustre de Füssen.

El mayor de los lagos, hoy día región preferida para los deportes de agua, el rey de Baviera no podía, en el siglo décimonono preverlo: el **Forggensee**, en efecto, se ha formado al través del encauzamiento del Lech por una central eléctrica. El embalse llega casi hasta Füssen, la antigua ciudad a los pies de los Alpes de Lechtal. Es sobrepujado por el **Hohes Schloss**, el castillo más antiguo de la región. Fue construído en el siglo décimotercero y servía de residencia veraniega a los obispos príncipes. Hoy contiene una colección de pinturas y el Juzgado.

Photo at bottom: Winter evening at Hohenschwangau castle
Photo on p. 69: King Ludwig's fairytale Neuschwanstein castle

Figura abajo: Noche de invierno al castillo de Hohenschwangau.
Figura p. 69: El fabuloso castillo de Neuschwanstein del Rey Ludwig.

Page 70, top left: Portrait of King Ludwig II
Page 70 top right: Neuschwanstein castle
Page 70, bottom: Neuschwanstein castle and Hohenschwangau
castle with the Alpsee
Page 71
Top: Neuschwanstein: throne room
Bottom: Murals (left: Tristan's farewell to Isolde; right:
Walther von der Vogelweide)

Figura página 70 arriba a la izquierda: Retrato del Rey Ludwig II.
Figura página 70 arriba a la derecha: Castillo de Neuschwanstein
Figura abajo: Los castillos de Neuschwanstein y Hohenschwangau
con el Alpsee.
Página 71:
Figura arriba: Neuschwanstein: sala del trono.
Figuras abajo: Pinturas sobre la pared (a la izquierda el adios
de Tristano a Isotta; a la derecha: Walther von der Vogelweide).

Large photo: Marienbrücke (St. Mary's bridge) over Pöllat gorge
Plate 1: Neuschwanstein: study
Plate 2: Neuschwanstein: singers' room
Plate 3: Neuschwanstein: bedroom

Figura grande: El puente de María, arriba la garganta de Pöllat.
Figura 1: Estudio de Neuschwanstein.
Figura 2: Sala de los cantantes de Neuschwanstein.
Figura 3: El dormitorio de Neuschwanstein.

Top: Hohenschwangau Castle
Bottom left: The Lion Fountain in the castle courtyard of Hohenschwangau
Bottom right: Tasso's bedroom in Hohenschwangau castle

Figura arriba: El castillo de Hohenschwangau.
Figura abajo a la izquierda: La Fuente de los Leones en el patio del castillo Hohenschwangau.
Figura abajo a la derecha: La habitación de Tasso en el Castillo de Hohenschwangau.

Füssen

Top: Musical Theater Neuschwanstein with the two Castles of King Ludwig
Large photo, bottom: On the Forggensee near Füssen
Small photo: Boat trip on the Forggensee
Photos on the right side:
Large photo, top: Füssen on the banks of the Lech, with High castle
Small photo, top: Tegelberg cableway, with view of Füssen
Large photo, bottom: Füssen pedestrian precint
Small photo, bottom: View of castle courtyard

Arriba: Teatro Musical Neuschwanstein con los dos castillos del Rey Ludwig.
Figura grande abajo: Sobre al Forggensee en Füssen.
Figura pequeña: Excursión sobre el Forggensee.
Página de la derecha:
Figura grande, arriba: Füssen sobre las orillas del Lech con el Castillo Alto.
Figura pequeña arriba: El funicular del Tegelberg con vistas sobre Füssen.
Figura grande abajo: La zona peatonal de Füssen.
Figura pequeña abajo: Vista sobre el patio del castillo.

From Oberjoch to Lake Constance

The Bavarian Allgäu starts in Füssen, and we will follow it along the edge of the Tannheim and Allgäu Alps to Lake Constance. We start our trip in Oberjoch, reached either from the Tannheim Valley (Austria) or by crossing the Jungholz and Unterjoch; leaving behind us the numerous hairpin bends on the pass road, we descend to **Hindelang,** turn north in Sonthofen to the Allgäu Alps, and visit **Oberstdorf.**

Oberstdorf (the highest village) lies in a narrow valley between Breitach, Stillach and Trettach, surrounded by high peaks like the Nebelhorn (2224 m), Höfats (2258 m), Fellhorn (2037 m), Mädelegabel (2649 m) and Belser (1653 m). Today, the Oberstdorf spa is one of the major winter sports resorts in Europe. Numerous cableways and an excellent footpath network provide access to one of the most beautiful parts of the Allgäu Alps.

From Oberstdorf we take the German Alps road, passing through **Immenstadt** and **Oberstaufen**, to **Lindau on Lake Constance**, the westernmost town in the Bavarian Allgäu. The island town, which was mentioned for the first time in the 9th century, still has one of the best-preserved mediaeval town centres in Bavaria.

◆

En Füssen empieza el Allgäu Bavarés que recorremos a lo largo de los márgenes de Tannheimer y Allgäuer Alpen hasta el Lago de Costanza. Empezamos nuestro camino en Oberjoch, o desde Tannheimer Tal (Austria) o llegando desde Unterjoch desde el valle de Jungholz; dejando a nuestras espaldas las numerosas curvas de la carretera, descendemos hasta **Hindelang** y a **Sonthofen** giramos hacia el norte en las Allgäuer Alpen y nos dirigimos a **Oberstdorf.**

Oberstdorf (= el pueblo más alto) se encuentra en un valle entre Breitach, Stillach y Trettach, y está rodeado de altos picos como el Nebelhorn (2224 m.), Höfars (2258 m.), Fellhorn (2037 m.), Mädelegabel (2649 m.) y Belser (1653 m.). Hoy la localidad climática de Oberstdorf es una de las más importantes de Europa por los deportes de invierno. Numerosos teleféricos y una extensa red de senderos permiten el acceso a una de las más bellas zonas de las Allgäuer Alpen.

Desde Oberstdorf, siguiendo la carretera alemana de los Alpes pasando por **Immenstadt** y **Oberstaufen** llegamos a **Lindau en el Lago de Costanza**, la ciudad más occidental del Allgäu bavarés. Aún hoy, la ciudad nombrada por primera vez en el siglo IX, es uno de los centros medievales mejor conservados de Baviera.

Plate 1: Oberjoch
Plate 2: Hindelang
Plate 3: Sonthofen

Figura 1: Oberjoch.
Figura 2: Hindelang.
Figura 3: Sonthofen.

Oberstdorf

Top: Oberstdorf, looking towards the Grosser Krottenkopf (2657 m)
Bottom left: The Heini-Klopfer ski-jumping platform in the Birgsau Valley
Bottom right: The Nebelhorn cableway summit station (2224 m)

Figura arriba: Oberstdorf con vista sobre el Großer Krottenkopf (2657 m.).
Figura abajo a la izquierda: El trampolín de salto Heini-Klopfer en el Valle de Birgsau.
Figura abajo a la derecha: El funicular de Nebelhorn (estación sobre la cima 2224 m.).

Top: Einödsbach with Mädelegabel (2645 m)
Bottom left: On the Fellhorn (1967 m)
Bottom right: S. Loretto's Sanctuary

Figura arriba: Einödsbach con Mädelegabel (2645 m.).
Figura abajo a la izquierda: Sobre el Fellhorn (1967 m.).
Figura abajo a la derecha: Santuario de San Loretto.

Top: Mt. Gerstruben (1154 m). View of Mt. Höfats (2258 m)
Bottom left: Breitachklamm near Oberstdorf
Bottom right: "Vieh-Scheid" (Transhumance)

Figura arriba: Gerstruben (1154 m.). Vista sobre Höfats (2258 m.).
Figura abajo a la izquierda: Breitachklamm en Oberstdorf.
Figura abajo a la derecha: "Vieh Scheid" (Trashumancia)